SPITTING IMAGE

Crab Orchard Series in Poetry
First Book Award

SPITTING IMAGE

POEMS BY

KARA VAN DE GRAAF

Crab Orchard Review &
Southern Illinois University Press
Carbondale

Southern Illinois University Press
www.siupress.com

Printed in the United States of America

21 20 19 18   4 3 2 1

The Crab Orchard Series in Poetry is a joint publishing
venture of Southern Illinois University Press and *Crab
Orchard Review*. This series has been made possible by the
generous support of the Office of the President of Southern
Illinois University and the Office of the Vice Chancellor
for Academic Affairs and Provost at Southern Illinois
University Carbondale.

Editor of the Crab Orchard Series in Poetry: Jon Tribble
Judge for the 2016 First Book Award: Jennifer Richter

Cover illustration: *Girls 6*, by Gemma Antón, 2014

Library of Congress Cataloging-in-Publication Data
Names: Van de Graaf, Kara, author.
Title: Spitting image / poems by Kara van de Graaf.
Other titles: Poems. Selection
Description: Carbondale : Crab Orchard Review & Southern
    Illinois University Press, 2018. | Series: Crab Orchard Series
    in Poetry
Identifiers: LCCN 2017037815 | ISBN 9780809336623
    (softcover) | ISBN 9780809336630 (e-book)
Subjects: | BISAC: POETRY / American / General. | SOCIAL
    SCIENCE / Women's Studies.
Classification: LCC PS3622.A585358 A6 2018 | DDC
    811/.6—dc23
LC record available at https://lccn.loc.gov/2017037815

Printed on recycled paper. ♻

This paper meets the requirements of ANSI/NISO Z39.48-
    1992 (Permanence of Paper) ∞

CONTENTS

*

Things keep happening. I keep sewing
the seam of the ripped shirt, the needle

sawing back and forth, its slow way
of binding. The cardinal flying,

the sound of traffic on the avenue,
drivers muted in their cars, safe

behind glass. And you in the kitchen
at the big basin washing potatoes,

the brush back and forth until they're clean,
until they hardly have skin at all. Things

keep happening. No one stops anyone else
on the street, no one notices small signs:

the light bulb stuttering out, a flash of red
blowing across the sidewalk, the subtle,

unnoticeable coming of silence, easily,
like the movement into sleep. My palm

working, the silver needle. The raw potatoes
glistening in the basin, clean and white as eyes.

I wait to hear her fall asleep,
hide under the bed. My mother,
with her dark hair pinned flat,

my mother like a small bird
suspended above. What separates us:
thin planks, a mattress, soft things

she uses to comfort herself. I press
my palms flat against wood. Now
she shifts, sits up on the bed. I see only

the shadowed pillars of her feet, feel
only my breath, its calculable measure.
I try not to give myself away.

When she settles, her presence ticks
away slowly, hangs in the air.
I listen to the bed, its creaking

as she starts to slip off. I am so still
now, waiting. Any moment
I am going to disappear.

That coy meeting which is beginning
and ending all at once, anatomical

oversight, no name for it I know.

What would she sound like? A good girl
speaks only when spoken to, is flat

like a watercolor, which means

the light is always hitting the same place
on her hair, her hands are always folded,

like a reflex, as if they are hiding something:

if you can't say the words, you secret them
into your hand, little whispers she collects

like thread, or fancy buttons

off her mother's dresses, each one round
as an oyster pearl. Mother says, *this*

is what ladies know. There is a price

for speaking, for the lips parting. The mouth
has to break every time.

LA MONSTRUA VESTIDA

after Juan Carreño de Miranda, 1680

There isn't room for anything

else: all body, costumed in red,

fabric stretched over wood,

entire width of a canvas.

Only six but she weighs as much

as a full-grown man. Round-bellied,

surly, she is part of a collection

of anomalies, like a pug-faced

dog or a dwarf, a yellow-crowned

parrot, its throat such vivid orange

the court had never seen it before.

In this museum, too, she is an anomaly,

a body I half-recognize as my own,

a familiar I project horror onto

like a mother. Every brushstroke

threatens to unravel us: where the ribs

of her dress unfasten; where

her pursed lips, almost elegant,

obscure her teeth—stitches pulling

in a seam. Ladies at court couldn't help

but love her, their figures appearing,

by contrast, that much closer

to perfection. Each hand clasps a globe

of fruit, tinged red where tiny breasts

might be, as though a parody

of the ideal woman. Little jolts

of sweetness she holds on to until

the posing is over and they find

their way into the stomach, that place

where we bury things until they become us.

I offer myself to her, not
                  with perfume, not with the sin

of too much flesh, but merely because
            I am the only breathing thing

in half a mile. After swimming, prone
                on the dock's planks, I feel the spandex

suit clinging like a carapace.
            Underneath the deck, shallows

thicken with marsh grass, shaded lodes
            of snails drift and pull

into themselves at the slightest rough.
            The fly hounds me, her hum and drone in my ear.

I understand; we always want
            what we see in front of us.

Remember what it was like underwater:
            the surface distant, unreachable, like listening

to the whole earth through a glass held up
            to a door. She moves to land

on my shoulder and I let her, wait
            only a moment before the mandible's sting.

It's my choice to be broken open.
            Only the females bite for blood.

In the dry months the men are gone
to work and the days set in like a kind

of machine. I look for anything to help
me bide, for what is familiar: bluegrass

perfuming the heat, raven's guttural choke.
The spiders' nests meshing in pine. One hot

morning the webs will all break, hang
from the tree limbs ataxic. Bodies

will trickle down the branch, a dark strain
of sap. Then the nest will burst. I'll move

close, watch one of the clutter, legs ghostly
as the veins of an angiographed brain. But now,

how the strands settle on the needles like a white
veil, water sequinning the netted surface. Knitted

houses that only pretend to transparency, that foil
my prying eyes. Some births can only happen in private.

THE POETICS OF FATNESS

I understand.

Everything about me

is supposed to get smaller,

get pared down and excised,

a single syllable struck from a line.

This is economy of language, not supply

and demand, but demand and demand and

all that white space enjambed. But I cannot fit

inside this stanza, this airless room around the words.

Must everyone inked be ideal, blurred over, appear in Photoshop

perfection? I am open to your suggestion. How do I fit this body inside

this poem? Will you look at it? Can I make a line break, or is even that an assault?

Do I have to go beyond the boundary of one page, span the meeting of the binding,

that border which pens one thought from another, keeps each poem safe? Do I have to lose

all restraint—be endlessly maximalist, until the paper is black, until the ream is cut at the center

of a letter? Would that make it better? Or is the nature of poetry that we all take a loss? And then, where

do I stop, what do I cut off to leave you a little bit hungry, wanting a little more of my music inside your mouth?

EPITHALAMIUM

In my family, we eat
our words like bread.

This is how we have not come
to speak of you.

This is how I learn
some things should not be spoken of.

Let us pretend we might have existed
in the same space, that your life
would not mean my death by omission.

Sometimes we shock a nerve so much it dies.

If you had not gone to war. If you had
come back. If she was

some other woman, in some other life:

the dresses fine and made
of cotton, the roses on the table
big as fists.

Deep
in the roundness
of her cells, my grandmother
designed me.
If you are conceived
in a trap, you are born
in a trap. She is dead now,
though still she pulls and pulls me
with admonitions
and advice, her measuring
tape and scales, as if I am something dirty
that needs
to be boiled pure. She never
spoke, not about anything,
just moved.
She believed
in the present.
In her later years, I caught
her writing secret words
in pencil—
moments she didn't want to lose
as her brain misfired
and choked, as her body
undid its own future.
What a big body, what
fat veins animated her arms,
my arms.
Bovine, we let
others feed on us, milking
our feelings and intellect.

How dearly she wanted
to press herself over me, duplicate
me, erase
the shiny trap she made,
which I'm still inside.

The fields suffer
them, pare the millet
to seed like an offering
of pearls. Their nests

are lined with dry grass,
twigs, the bits of twine
we use to bind the bodies
of kept fowl before

we strip them to the white
skin. In the hard season,
we all keep our own
treasures. At dawn I see them

moving in and out
of the branches, a single
breath in the old oak's
chest. Year after year

they linger even when
the woods go buzzing
with migratory wings,
that strange hunger

for movement that presses
the flocks, makes them
yield. Starlings keep, massed,
a stubborn thought rustling

in the brain. Stay when the earth
hardens. When the boys whip
their stones, the snow,
the white, shot with blood.

Little pocket, two side doors
to the brain where outside

and inside meet. It is always
working, even in the dampered

night: metal bedsprings, the old
house settling, the white fridge

lumbering to life. Or your body,
that factory, with its beating

and its breathing—all the cogs
and networks you hear

inside yourself, the white
noise of your body

like a sudden change
in pressure in a plane,

the popping and squeaking
a protest to altitude.

And while you rise,
the surface is being written

below: the cities, their cars,
the countryside with its neat

patchwork. How quickly
they become small, fragile,

too far to hear, encased
by the glass of the window, as in

a museum, its uniformed guard,
the finger pressed to his lips.

WASHING

At the creek by the campsite, my hands work
the soiled shirt, mill it against the board

that keeps on stuttering out its one word.
When I was a child, I heard my mother

make this sound, her fingers lacing
into wet cloth. I beat my own chest, thumped

my palms in time to her rhythm, bleating out
broken music as she rubbed the sheets,

the collars, her metal bucket rocking. Spiraled
with soap. I sang my music and my mother's body

kept pivoting up and back at the hip, as if all
the washing were one long motion that didn't start

or stop, as if she were rendering, with her cracked
hands, what was pure from the earth.

SPLITTING IMAGE

I have my mother's
eyes, I have
        my mother's nose,
        the Weiss family
nose she calls it.
I see its echo
        on my face
        like a photograph
xeroxed until
it is all grain, features
        present but out
        of focus. On
the radio I listen
to doctors who
        thought the placenta
        could not be crossed.
There was the
mother and then
        there was the child,
        alive but adjacent,
like two countries.
And now they look
        in the blood and
        see it isn't true.
Fetal cells stay alive
in the mother,

are not attacked

though the DNA is foreign.

This happens

even if the child

isn't born. Even if

it is a map

for someone

who never was.

Our flesh is never

our flesh alone.

My mother changed

her name when she

married and I changed

mine, though we still

carry that older name

written in our features.

They avoid erasure

even though *Weiss* means

covered over

and blanked, *Weiss*

means forgotten.

Sometimes,

it means bleached,

the way photographers

dodge a dark spot

on a negative, reveal

the architecture

of an image underneath.

I trussed the hen and cut the breast
clean, pliable, soft with cartilage.
I thought my mouth could swallow it
whole, but the bone went brittle, broke
through the skin of my neck like two
thorns. Its prongs scissored out above
my clavicle. Windpipe split in a perfect *Y*.
When I speak, each phrase kaleidoscopes,
modifies, a duet of whispers I lip into air.
I sound sweet when I want to be bitter. I bite
back my anger's flare. My voice box grows
into an echo chamber, buzzes double-alive.
Forgive me, I must say everything twice:
once to punish, once to entice.

*

FLOATING GIRL

The men in the little boat discovered her
like an island erupted in night. Early morning
she drew, as if by magic, toward the surface.

They saw the sway of arms, the cursived hair
that wrote in time to the current. They saw
the map of veins—the shadowed skin where blood

had banked—and knew. She'd made a bed of coral
and anemone, blossoms circling her like a meadow
wreath. And all day the coral came to understand

the shape of her body like an argument, the soft turn
of its logic: swathe of prickled flesh on her calves,
balletic curve of the hip's bone. Weeks and weeks,

until the girl was more than a girl, ribboned through
as she was with coral's bone. Until she rose to meet
the boat, remade—as men, each season, remake the fields.

Nothing miraculous. Maybe colder
than you thought, maybe darker,

maybe so dim you have to give up
seeing altogether, the way over centuries

certain fish on the bottoms of caves turned
pale as corpses, forfeited the luxury

of eyes. But it wouldn't matter. Here,
the surface is all lies, the moon halved

and distant, some neon streetlamp
that comes on like clockwork.

There's no mistaking the world
is shifting. The surface gluts back

on itself all day long, rocking,
as if trying to remember something

simple, something close—the time of day,
the drawn out syllables of its own name.

But the lesson of water is forgetting,
is taking any name at all. You know this

like a promise in the grayed brain,
a message bearing over you in waves

until you are swayed, until
you yield, malleable, and fine as silt.

The Iroquois believe that an animal seen in a dream is a sign.

i.

Before they kill the hogs
they castrate them.
This is so the drive to mate
with a sow won't ruin
the meat. The best
pigs have the least fat,
are only slightly
jowly. The most humane
method is to jolt them
insensible, feed the current
right into the seizing brain.
Before the shock hits
you can hear them scream,
heads upturned, aggressively
snouty, like the faces of the boys
in the Jeep Wrangler who held
up their noses with a finger,
snorted into my pink pig face.

ii.

As a child I had a recurring dream
I was being eaten alive
by pigs. Each time it returned

I thought I had hidden myself,
this time, I won't be found.
But then I heard the high sounds

of their snouts, tasted the dark
earth and the blood. They were
not ordinary in their pigginess,

red in the eyes, demons,
the drift of them bristling
with thick, black hairs.

I don't know why the dream
stopped coming, or why
it seemed to come back

like a loop buried in my brain
where their tusks always rooted
me out like sweetness, like a prize.

iii.

If I had the mind of an animal,

                               it would be a pig.

That web of synapses firing so terrifyingly close

to our surface, smarter than dogs and chimps,

almost human in the eyes.

                        We love them

because they are so willing to accept

what we offer from the bottom,

                           the waste

and the scraps, empty husks.

                      They live for them,

squealing in delight. In the mysteries of their stomachs

they become the parts of us we cast off, the rotting

and the rinds, just as

                    the Iroquois chose

to eat the fresh hearts of their enemies so that

they could love them

                    and conquer them at the same time.

Above all, what I have feared is love.
I have been afraid of my body, of its weakness,
its need that feels like a pail filling slowly
with milk. I have watched kids at the teat,

how their mouths are formed to pull
every sweetness toward them, to suck
the body tired, the nipple raw and jewel-like.
Who would choose such a bitter ornament?

Who could understand a creature that gladly
admits anything that arrives at its gates?
I have put my hand to the soft stomach
of a doe, and I have heard her throat

bleating in the labor. I prefer to let the rod
do my speaking. I prefer to let them call my name.

POEM ON THE END OF A LURE

I count to ten, wait for the sunfish
to stop fighting for air; terrible

to need only what is so close.
Here, the belly won't resist

the sharp end of a knife, opens pink
as a girl's mouth. I take the fish

to water and rinse the inside clean,
break apart the body's small order.

Strip the silvered scales and side-fins
that fanned so beautifully

when it could swim, billowing out
like a dress against wind. I snap

the line again, almost invisible except
for its sharpening of light, send the lure

back below the river's surface. I wait,
cloistered on the banks, my feet pitted

against open tree roots for balance,
their dark curves serpentine, arched

as a dorsal on the fish's boned back.
Slick, those thick knots spreading right

into water. I can't help but love a thing
that understands what to expose.

THE FISHERMAN

In Volendam, we acted
like tourists, though only I
was the stranger—an American
with a Dutch husband.

We dressed up at the photo booth:
a young fisherman and his wife.
A net slung over his shoulder,
he smoked a pipe. She wore wooden shoes.

We walked back
along the harbor and laughed
at the photos. How outside
ourselves we were. A pelican
landed dockside, stopped,
gullet full and draining.
I had never seen one up close.

I thought about his catch:
invisible, gap-mouthed,
pressing through
the throat—

they had found themselves a vessel
and belonged to him now.

When the house shudders you hear
it here first, all the fine things give up

their hiding, tremble as they settle
against the shelves. Everything has

a place. The champagne flutes'
sharp inhale, the goblets' swollen

bellies bowing out one
by one down the line. So much glass

which more than any other
substance has learned to lie, pulling

all its matter from somewhere
else: the painted walls, the curtain,

a stray flash of color
through the doorway that startles

them all to life. In the drawers
the silver stacks and nestles

against itself, refuses to resist
the body of its mate.

Every spoon, every knife
submits so completely it reduces

to a thin sterling line, holds
even against the drawer's

slam. Don't believe all things
disobey when given the chance.

PORTRAIT OF MY MOTHER AS CAPTAIN JAMES COOK

> *The constitution of his body was robust, inured to labour, and
> capable of undergoing the severest hardships. His stomach bore,
> without difficulty, the coarsest and most ungrateful food.*
>
> —Captain John Bolton King

For a whole week, I visited the shore,
red kernels of shells mounding in my fingers

like beads, like small seeds natives drove
into the ground with one thumb until

they sprouted up green again. I tried to capture
you on the page, but each entry felt vaguer

than the last. Yesterday, I trapped a fish
and skinned it whole. No time here to blade

the body down, bones burring the catch
even as it blisters in fire. When you eat you pick

them carefully, little needles that cut
against sweet pink flesh.

Creatures of the sea, our bones are wed to water, our teeth
make gifts of themselves. White hills of salt.
Away from land's umbilical pull, sand-strangled grass
on the dunes, we become ourselves again.
Skin phosphoring against the sweat-varnished decks,
our thighs slimmed, petaled over with pink. And what miracles
radiate from our joints, make us forget brine of meat,
the festering shit. At night, in water's cradle, our eyes sink
into themselves, gray as the flash of a silver coin.
All the old scars return, flower open like new wounds.

Everything is sweet: smell of pitch-tar, saliva that honeys
the mouth, a parched disc of tack crumbling like dust
over our tongues. Each morning we palm one, brittle,
its surface cratered—a small moon cupped in the hand.
The ship's hold is dark. What happens there happens beyond
our eyes, life boring suddenly through. Snakelike bodies
honeycomb the stores, our bellies, ream us to the core. All day
we feel them mine us, like earth, one dark tunnel at a time.

If I press its metal ring to my face,
        the lid of my eye opens
            like a door.
Fingers scoped around the body
        I make grow thinner
           and thinner,

a funnel punctuated with vertebrae
        of brass. I want to find
           them on the shore,
my left eye squinted dormant, blind
        stone at the center of a plum.
           In the lens

they look small, like children herding together
        in the schoolyard, setting up
           imaginary house.
I watch them gather invisible
        things. I wonder if they can feel
           my eyes touching

them like a briar pricking the flesh,
        or the splinter-tip of an arrow
           in the body
of a bird, the wing that stops
        catching air and lets the earth
           pull it back.

Whales can create sounds in excess of 180 decibels, louder than
a rocket launch, that carry underwater for more than a mile.
—BBC Earth

Speak, mighty head, and tell us the secret thing that is in thee.
—Herman Melville

At the Natural History Museum, I stand inside—
the great skull tipped upward, the ribs circling me

     like a gate. You giant, you patron saint
     of taking up space. Just the skeleton hangs

from reinforced steel cording, the mammal
in sum too massive to survive air. And while

     I fit my small body inside its bones,
     the living ones swim still underwater, each one

a blue organ of the earth that beats and beats,
circulates over hundreds of miles. They live

     by refusing to be quiet, by remaking the world
     with their sound. In the open waters of Alaska,

whales migrate each year with their calves,
hunt sardines, silver gasps, all one mind

and so much flesh. Whales build a funnel of speech

inside their skulls, a song they can shoot with

that stops the shoal's swarming, pushes it

into frenzy. In the museum, cloaked in this body,

I feel my loudness tunneling up like stunned

fish shunting toward the surface,

ready to be taken gently in the mouth, ready

to meet the weapon they were made for.

Red matchstick I thumb   alive and send
ahead of me through the dark   little emissary,
little locket of light   that lets the eye wick

to the cellar's walls, the green   line of mineral
where flood rises up   waist-high. Groundwater
seethes through cracks   in the mortar, laces
between stones,   their flat smooth faces
already buried.   All night I ferry

buckets to the surface. All night   my fingers
seam together and I climb,   my sleeping
like one long flight   of stairs, my bucket

like a mouth that won't drown.   In the end,
I envied the bucket.   The way all things
that are empty   want to be filled.

*

No promised land. No paradise with yellow
fruits marring the dusky beach, frills
of an unfamiliar plant rippling out

like a clitoris. Not even a great nothing
to discover, suicide cliff-fall to gurney,
its wet mist rising opium-white.

We curse the maps, finger their crossed
latitudes that hatch over us like a cage.
When the world ends it just keeps going.

*

It just keeps going, the end of the world
hatching over me like a cage. At each latitude
I am cursed, my fingers find the edge of a map.

My face rises, misty and opium-white,
my body held on a gurney. I discover suicide
is not even a great nothing. Not like my clitoris

rippling out, unfamiliar, a plant that frills
a dusky beach. When we married, nothing
fruited like a yellow paradise. No promised land.

CONTRAPPOSTO

Yet it is less the horror than the grace
    Which turns the gazer's spirit into stone.
        —Percy Bysshe Shelley, "On the Medusa of
    Leonardo da Vinci in the Florentine Gallery"

All day long I touched
        the broken faces of men.

I watched their features crumble,
        a chevron gone from a lip,

the side of a head smashed off
        leaving half a gunshot

eye. Ancients, I have entertained
        your arguments and illusions.

I have listened, but I still see
        your gods all knocked apart:

divine back to human,
        human back to stone.

That night the August heat
        conjured an animal stench

in the streets of the old city,
        punishing us as we slept

near the cramped window. I dreamed
        of our elders' sick love

of symmetry. Persuaded,
      I believed my own face

was remade in stone—cracks
      rising up like welts over my jaw.

In the morning I woke and
      you found me no longer beautiful.

In the dressing room at Macy's,
I run into all my old bodies.
We are reunited when I hear them
shuffling in the walls, sense them
beneath the dirty carpet. Their hips
lurching out of drywall. Their breasts
swelling against the concrete floor.
I congratulate one on her thin legs.
We commiserate about side-boob.
We try on dresses from the junior's section
and laugh. Relive our proms, our red-haired
date who cried the whole night
about that other girl. We kiss. Arm-wrestle.
Bitch-slap. Wish we were never born.
When we part we look at each other longingly,
doe-eyed. The way two mirrors,
when you put them opposite, reflect
each other forever and ever.

Three hits to loosen the crook
of her spine, five to widen the reach
of her thighs. They sharpened
their blades and tapped around
the prize, worked until their eyes
stung red with rust. The hammers
cleaved the rock, their bodies cleaved
and spit, though she wouldn't
come free. When they saw how
she fused to the bedrock, how
her hair veined through the walls
like quartz, they dropped their axes
and watched her. One by one, their cells,
touched with oxygen, turned on like lights.

Certain individuals on six month flights have lost as much as 20 percent of bone mass throughout their lower extremities.
—Dr. Jay Shapiro, National Space
Biomedical Research Institute

The planet sleeping
and distant, strung over

with lights like an old
circuit board—I forget
I have escaped its pull.

My body lurched free,
for the first time in its living.

In the fading atmosphere,
the land reduces mile by mile
to a topographic map of itself.

Up here, I live by my own
rhythms. I black out

the circular windows.
I hitch my body to anything
that will hold me, press

the straps over my ankles
when I sleep to keep

from losing myself
in the night. The doctors say
I am becoming less than I was.

     That my bones are hollowing
     at their center. This is the price

I accept for weightlessness.
For feeling my hand grasping
air, buoyed to nothing.

As if Einstein were wrong, after
       all, as if the body were a black
hole that swallows and swallows
       but does not give back. The body
so lonely it needs to make everything
       part of itself, creates itself
through annihilation.
       Everything that is not *it*
will become *it*: crumbs
       on the tablecloth, the cake,
the plate that holds the cake,
       the wheat, small birds living
in a field, your field, your face,
       words stolen from your mouth.
As if all things beautiful
       must be sucked out
of living, must purr in the stomach,
       like the succulent fat at the marrow
of our bones, that centering
       that keeps the blood clean.
That millimeter of space that means
       all of us are apart, that means
we can never really touch
       anything, that quantum air
that strikes a distance between us
       in our airplane seats, in our beds
at night. Yes, I want that, too.

Carvings spine over the cabinet's front,
hairline, delicate as the scaffolding

of a wren's wing. And the etched case,
too, is the wren's patterned body;

its breastbone like a prow—
the Steinway's curved rim. I want

to hold the keys against my palm,
the same cleft of my hand where,

once, I held a small bird as it failed.
When it happened, I felt a door shut

in the chest, heavy as a glossed lid,
watched the eyes, still black, only

the way out was closed. And silence.
But before silence, a low sound flocking

the back of the throat, trailing off
the way I imagine the first key

on the lip of the piano might sound
if I struck it softly. If I let myself.

I thought I heard each strand separate,
each thread woven into the others
sheared away like a braid snipped

from the base of the neck. I couldn't see.
Sight doesn't belong to the dying. Still,
the pieces were falling, caught by wind

or gravity or the hands of a child reaching
for a token to remember. What else I heard:
the caw of a crow stretching away from me,

the startled body lifting before it knows
the axe is not for him. The long syllable
of the blade falling down its runners, screeching

within the track's groove. It is a trick
that any substance which grinds
against itself long enough is not destroyed

but made smoother, more pleasing.
I think my favorite animal is the crow.
It understands how to use a tool.

I searched for her all summer
        in the old house, her offspring
weaving their hairline streams
        across the kitchen tile, across

its pitted vinyl that intersected
        like stars. I could not find
her nest. I ran a rake
        along the flaking foundation,

tore the roots away where
        the house met the earth, and found
no breach. I sprayed and they returned.
        My husband ate like a monk

over a tacky tablecloth covered
        in ivy, everything zippered
in plastic, and yet their dark bodies,
        quivering with antennae, freckled

our feet. It was by accident
        I found the den, nestled between
the two frames of the attic window,
        a spot of white at the end of the ledge

like the follicle of a stray hair.
        Between the panes, I saw her
black body—her rounded
        thorax, her shiny, ringed abdomen—

and thought how many times
        she had labored to repeat herself, how
her glistening eggs each held a baby
        like the glazed-over pupil of an eye.

ECHO CHAMBER

Škocjan Caves, Slovenia

      I am a thousand steps
under the earth with my mother,
         the cave gestating
   in our minds, still only
imaginary. We climb the stairway

built for tourists,
   but still we step carefully,

where explorers clawed their passage
      down, not knowing
    if there was
anybody on the other side
     listening for their tremor.

Down
     in the belly,
our bodies leaning against each other,
     I confront it: this place
    is a machine
making itself over
    and over. Stalactites
and stalagmites reach
      toward each other, trying
  to close the gap between them.

The guide warns us
not to touch them:
        our fingers can set
   the process back
          hundreds of years.

If you say a word here,
        it comes back to you.
The louder you say it,
           the more it comes back.

Before it was contaminated,
        this was a closed system,
Now even
           little things can be
   disruptive, like the light
from our headlamps
       that makes visible

what was never visible, spurs
       the green moss
      on the rocks to grow
and feed. The body
       is not a closed system,
but like my mother
          before me, I keep trying
   to close it. I contract
and expand, like the water
      starved of minerals.

In this dim chamber
         I can feel her feeding
     on me like a thin film
     of algae in the light, can see
we harbor the same defect—

something that was there
even before we were there,
                    before we were human

and our brains made us part
            with our bodies.

MY APOLOGY

When you're at work, I take out your old toothbrush
and dip it in bleach. In my dirty Purdue sweatshirt,

I kneel in the bathtub, grinding the bristles
back and forth on the discolored grout.

The lines turn crimson from iron in the water
and crack a bit near the seams, like red gums.

It bothers you. Over an hour, the bleach does its work,
makes the caulking look almost new. Each time

I check, the shower is whiter, like a scene
from a time-lapse camera. I don't know

how else to show you. In the evening, I read you my poem
about the bird. You nod. How can you ask me why

I don't put our life together in words?
Everything I say is addressed to you.

SCHEVENINGEN

It's easy to be deceived—
a sudden flash that is not
the sun, a chill that feels

like fire. The air's infected,
carries the sound of the sea,
a constant murmur that presses

just below my hearing.
During the war, the Dutch
used the name of the city

as a shibboleth to root out
the Germans hiding there.
Now, preserved hotels

loom on the sand like mirages,
windows giving back
the world only in blue,

only flushed with sky.
When I need words,
I can no longer make them,

my mouth forgetting itself.
In the old streets, blocks of buildings
yawn open at the core,

a whole city gone slack in the jaw.

BURNED GIRL

Her body drapes neatly
across the doorstep like a gift

someone left. Face up, she reclines
in permanent flinch. The fingers curl

uncannily, almost fused, joined,
because nothing here is singular,

nothing separate: arm dug into
the walled ribs, blue silk shirt

fading in and out of flesh.
There is nobody to testify,

nobody to say it happened
suddenly, or the flames wicked

to her body, outlined it in relief;
or to say her arms welled

open, to say the cloud of fire.
Like she was moving into embrace.

No one can tell what her words were
at the end or if there were words.

Or if there was only silence
feeding silence like air.

CONTROLLED BURN

I mark the trunk with chalk. My fingers
stain neon, the sign I leave the men
to show them what is expendable.

Though every tree is flawed:
alder with a mummified arm, redwood
found hollow, debris tunneled into the center

like a hive. Sometimes death is the only way
to stay alive. Sequoias germinate
under the black stamp of fire. Sires

survive to carry the char. If I stay
with them and mark my own chest
like a door, would I be tender?

I read the scorched
wood like code, beams

and joists blackened
with the signs of sparks—

light stammered
out into the private

dark for no one. No eyes,
just the raw wood's

resined whorl, its circular
logic. My hand plumbs

the ribbing in the walls,
traces the rough grain

that gathers and parts
around the plank's knotting.

Encases it like a stunted
child. I try to feel

the coppered veins, spliced,
the ceramic joints that bind

them before they plunge
below. My fingers

surface, marked with black,
though the riggings hang limp.

I listen for the wire's spit
and trigger before I touch,

a language that would hiss
through my body, hand

to hand, blue me over,
pry me from my every pinning.

NOTES

"La Monstrua Vestida": The painting, which now hangs in Museo del Prado, depicts Eugenia Martínez Vallejo, a curiosity in the court of King Charles II.

"Lower Animals": The practice of ritual consumption of the heart in eighteenth-century Iroquois tribes is described in Peggy Reeves Sanday's *Divine Hunger: Cannibalism as a Cultural System* (Cambridge University Press, 1986), 125.

"Portrait of My Mother as Captain James Cook": The epigraph is taken from *The Voyages of Captain James Cook*, volume 2.

"Giants of the Sea": The epigraph from Melville appears in *Moby-Dick*, chapter 70, "The Sphynx." The poem is inspired by the blue whale skeleton in the Natural History Museum in London.

"Dream with Water beneath the Floorboards": This poem is for Ryan Richardson.

"Spaceflight": The epigraph comes from a 2001 article on NASA's website.

"Echo Chamber": This poem is for my mother, Cheryl.

"Scheveningen": This poem is for Dennis van de Graaf.

ACKNOWLEDGMENTS

I would like to thank the editors of the following publications, where these poems, sometimes in earlier versions, first appeared:

Adroit Journal: "Portrait of My Mother as the Virgin Queen"

AGNI: "The Doubles," "Lower Animals"

Alaska Quarterly Review: "Epithalamium"

Bellingham Review: "My Mother's Pantry," "Poem Wired with Knob-and-Tube"

Birmingham Poetry Review: "Spyglass"

Colorado Review: "My Apology"

Crazyhorse: "Sonnet with a Wishbone in the Throat"

Gettysburg Review: "Splitting Image"

Indiana Review: "Poem in the Corner of a Young Girl's Mouth," "Spitting Image"

The Journal: "Burned Girl"

Linebreak: "Dream with Water beneath the Floorboards"

Massachusetts Review: "Southern Gothic"

Meridian: "Madame la Guillotine," "Poem Traveling in a Circuit," "Spaceflight"

Michigan Quarterly Review: "Queen Ant"

Mid-American Review: "Starlings in Winter"

New England Review: "*La Monstrua Vestida*"

New South: "Poem on the End of a Lure"

Ninth Letter: "Poem in the Eardrum," "Poem on the Verge of Interruption"

Passages North: "Excavated Girl," "Horsefly"

Quarterly West: "Controlled Burn," "Ode to Hardtack," "Ode to Sea Scurvy"

Southern Indiana Review: "Poem in the Shape of a Grand Piano"

Southern Review: "Portrait of My Mother as Captain James Cook"

Third Coast: "Floating Girl"

"Poem at the Bottom of the Allegheny River" was published in *Best New Poets 2010*, edited by Claudia Emerson. "The Doubles" was reprinted on Poetry Daily.

For generous financial and artistic support, I thank the Poetry Center of Chicago, the Vermont Studio Center, the New York State Summer Writers Institute at Skidmore College, the Squaw Valley Community of Writers, the Sewanee Writers' Conference, the University of Pittsburgh, the University of Wisconsin–Milwaukee, and Utah Valley University.

I am deeply grateful to my teachers and mentors, many of whom had a profound impact on the conception of this book. Many thanks to Brenda Cárdenas, Anne Frances Wysocki, Dennis Lynch, and Mary Jo Salter. In writing this collection, I am indebted in particular to Marianne Boruch, Lynn Emanuel, and Rebecca Dunham.

I would also like to express my thanks and appreciation to the many friends, colleagues, and loved ones who supported me personally and artistically during the drafting of this manuscript, especially Jennifer Kontny, Tobias Wray, Julie Nelson, Colleen Abel, and Dennis van de Graaf. Most of all, thank you to Richie Hofmann. This collection would not exist without you.

Finally, thank you to my family, given and chosen. This book is for you.

Other Books in the Crab Orchard Series in Poetry